STOP PROCRASTINATION NOW!

DEFEAT THE TIME OPPONENT AND ACHIEVE YOUR GOALS

Master the Art of Time Management,
Conquer & Defeat Procrastination,
and Boost Your Productivity

Sarah C. Johnson

TABLE OF CONTENTS

INTRODUCTION

Most of us have experienced a moment or two where we feel overwhelmed, there is so much to do, and the work keeps piling on. It doesn't matter whether you're a student, employee, business owner, or stay-at-home parent, everyone wishes that they had more time to get everything done. This endless pile of work is further compounded by everything else we are bombarded by: emails, text messages, social media notifications, and personal and professional relationships—the list is endless. However, is it time that you truly lack, or is procrastination the real problem? You see, some people are aware of their tendency to procrastinate, they might even embrace it, thinking it makes them more productive when they get things done last minute. Although, they also always imagine how much more they could have done if they didn't waste time. Others fail to recognize their procrastination entirely and just think that they have too much to do and too little time. At this point, some of this might sound familiar to you. Procrastination can be our ultimate time opponent if we let it. This is why we need a better understanding of procrastination, its forms, and what strategies we can use to overcome it.

This book will provide a blueprint for those who find themselves always putting off tasks, both big and small. We often fail to realize that procrastination isn't an issue of time management alone, but a complex network of habits, attitudes, and unresolved inner conflicts. Until we understand this network and how it affects our lives, we are unable to establish the necessary techniques and strategies to overcome them and achieve our goals. By carefully evaluating our current circumstances and reflecting on our past, we can determine the root of our procrastination and work toward eliminating it once and for all. It is not an easy process, but one that is achievable and extremely liberating. When you are free from procrastination, you are also free to achieve whatever you set your mind to.

In this book, I have put together information that will help you understand procrastination better—from the different forms to the psychology behind it, before delving into strategies that you can implement to manage your time better and boost your productivity in all spheres of your life. The structure of this book will also help procrastinators stay focused and motivated to continue their journey to becoming more productive. It is concise, to the point, and will not offer meaningless information that will cause you to be easily distracted. It is possible to overcome procrastination, and it is not part of your personality or an unchangeable character trait. You just have to know what causes it so that you can find your way to deal with it—and this book will help you do that. Are you ready to get started?

CHAPTER 1

UNDERSTANDING PROCRASTINATION —THE TIME OPPONENT

How much do you know about procrastination? We all have a general idea of what procrastination is, but it is actually so much more than we realize. It has varying effects and comes in different disguises, which often makes it harder to recognize. It is possible to live in complete ignorance of your own procrastination, with some people even identifying procrastination as productivity! How is this possible? Well, let's take a closer look at this time opponent.

THE NATURE OF PROCRASTINATION

Let's start by defining procrastination. It is considered to be the delay or the avoidance to complete tasks or decisions that need to be accomplished. Procrastination is essentially a voluntary action, and many people just think that it is just the way they are. However, it often leads to unnecessary stress, poor performance, and general dissatisfaction in people's lives—but they still can't quite break the habit. It is so deeply connected to our thinking and actions that until we truly understand the root cause of our procrastination, we cannot begin to overcome it.

Procrastination can also be attributed to several factors such as task aversion, perfectionism, fear of failure, and lack of self-confidence. Some people procrastinate to avoid tasks they find unpleasant, difficult, or even boring. For perfectionists, fear of making mistakes or not meeting the high standards they have for themselves can lead to delays. In other cases, procrastination may even be a symptom of underlying conditions like ADHD or depression. We will delve deeper into these in the next chapter, but it is clear to see that the nature of procrastination is not the same for everyone. What is the same is the fact that we continue to procrastinate even though we know that it is not good for us.

It is also not uncommon for individuals to believe that their procrastination is good for their productivity. Knowing that they don't have much time to meet a deadline spurs them into action and allows them to complete a task in half the time they had allocated to it. Some people who work in creative fields also prefer waiting until the last minute because they believe that it will spark creativity or they have more time to consider all their possible options. However, working in high-pressure situations and the stress that it entails is not good for one's health in the long run. Furthermore, people would probably provide work of a much higher quality if they worked under less pressure and had enough time to review and edit their work.

This is why we continue to procrastinate despite knowing that it is a flaw. The positive results make us think that maybe it's helping us. However, it hinders us from reaching our true potential both in our personal and professional lives. We have to recognize procrastination as the opponent that it is and stop believing that it helps us accomplish our goals because it really does not.

THE IMPACT OF PROCRASTINATION ON YOUR GOALS

Both long and short-term goals are essential in our lives. We need to have targets that we work toward and aim to improve. This ensures that we move in a forward trajectory and do not remain stagnant in different areas of our lives. This goes for personal, professional, and academic goals. Procrastination can also affect how we perceive goals and our attitude toward them as we tend to brush them aside instead of actively trying to accomplish them.

In our personal lives, there are goals that we wish to achieve whether we define them or not. We all strive to be better, develop stronger relationships, improve our talents, and develop new ones. However, if we continuously delay working on these areas because we never have time or because there is something else that needs our attention, we will never make progress. This means that our personal development and growth will be hindered. In turn, this will lead to feelings of low self-esteem and dissatisfaction in our lives. It will also change the way you think about achieving goals and will cause you to limit your goals as you think that anything larger would be impossible.

When it comes to academics, procrastination can have dire consequences. Students who consistently postpone studying, completing assignments, or preparing for exams often face lower grades, increased stress, and diminished learning outcomes (Girdhar et al., 2020). This can significantly affect their academic performance and when they cannot achieve their academic goals, other problems arise as well. Firstly, it can impact their mental health because they begin to feel as if they are a failure for not achieving their academic goals. Secondly, it also impacts their futures because it limits their opportunities and causes them to feel as if they are not adequate enough for certain employment opportunities.

Lastly, when it comes to professional goals, procrastination can lead to missed deadlines, reduced productivity, and poor work quality. It can undermine career advancement, as consistent delays can lead to a reputation for unreliability, damaging professional relationships and opportunities. Moreover, it can increase stress levels, leading to job dissatisfaction and a negative work-life balance. Thus, procrastination can negatively affect your chances of advancing your career and achieving greater success. It has a much larger impact on your life than you could have ever imagined. This is why it is crucial to find strategies that will help you stop procrastination before it is too late.

THE TRUE COST OF PROCRASTINATION

Procrastination does not just impact our goals—our overall well-being is also affected by it. It is capable of affecting our mental health, relationships, self-esteem, reputation, decision-making, and physical well-being if we let it. If we look at this in detail, we can begin to better understand the true cost of procrastination.

Mental Health

Procrastinators often experience stress, anxiety, and guilt associated with their delayed tasks. The constant cycle of delaying tasks and the resulting stress can lead to feelings of guilt and self-doubt, potentially exacerbating mental health conditions like depression and anxiety. In the long run, the persistent stress caused by procrastination can also lead to burnout, a state of mental, emotional, and physical exhaustion.

Relationships

The habit of delaying can create friction and resentment, as others may perceive the procrastinator as irresponsible or unreliable. If one consistently misses personal commitments or is always late, friends, family, and partners may feel disrespected or undervalued. Over time, these perceptions can damage relationships and lead to isolation.

Self-Esteem

Habitual procrastination can lead to a cycle of self-perpetuating negative self-image. This will be discussed more in the next chapter, where we look at the psychology of procrastination in more detail. However, to explain it briefly, procrastinators often feel a sense of shame about their behavior, leading to diminished self-esteem. This is something many of us are familiar with, along with the internalized belief or self-identification of being a procrastinator. Once this occurs, you almost embrace the behavior, making the habit harder to break.

Reputation

Procrastinators are known for being unreliable. They ask for extensions on deadlines, are late to events, and are always rescheduling appointments. As a result, they are not the first people to pop into someone's mind when they need help. Whether it be at work or in your personal life, people will be less likely to think of you as being capable of getting a task done on time. This limits the opportunities you have to prove yourself as a better employee, colleague, friend, partner, or family member.

Decision-Making

One of the biggest costs of procrastination is the negative influence it has on the decisions we make. Procrastinators tend to make poor decisions because they make last-minute decisions out of haste rather than considering the factors involved. Furthermore, procrastinating will make our emotions and thoughts mislead us when we make decisions. For example, because we believe that we are not capable of achieving more due to the way we procrastinate, we will be more likely to pass on opportunities that could be extremely beneficial to our development and improvement in the long term.

Physical Health

The chronic stress and anxiety associated with procrastination can lead to numerous health issues, including insomnia, digestive problems, headaches, and cardiovascular disease. Additionally, procrastination in health-related behaviors, like delaying medical check-ups or ignoring symptoms, can result in severe health consequences.

Therefore, the true cost of procrastination is far more extensive than it might initially appear. By realizing the cost, we can begin to start making the changes necessary to ensure a better future for ourselves. We can have the time necessary to establish the proper work/life balance we dream of and we can also be the best versions of ourselves if we overcome procrastination.

CHAPTER 2
THE PSYCHOLOGY OF PROCRASTINATION

Now that we know how procrastination affects us, it's time to discover the psychology behind it. Procrastination is not just something we do; it is deeply embedded in human cognition and emotion. Therefore, we procrastinate because of what we feel and what we think. It is essentially an automatic response to these internal factors, and automatic responses are basically the definition of habits. This makes procrastination a bad habit that needs to be broken—and to do that, you need to identify the causes, triggers, and patterns that allow it to manifest in your life. This chapter will help you do that.

THE PROCRASTINATION CYCLE: HOW IT FEEDS

The procrastination cycle can often feel impossible to escape from. It begins with an impending task or project that causes stress or discomfort. The natural response to this discomfort is avoidance, which is where our procrastination steps in. We put off the task in favor of immediate relief, choosing activities that are more enjoyable or less stressful. Therefore, the discomfort is pushed aside for another time. However, as we delay the task, the stress associated with it doesn't disappear. It builds up, making the task seem even more daunting than before. This leads to further procrastination, creating a feedback loop that keeps feeding itself. The irony is that while procrastination provides temporary relief, in the long run, it only amplifies stress and anxiety.

Thus, in order to stop procrastinating, you need to stop feeding the loop. To do this, you need to be aware of why you are avoiding the task. Where does this discomfort come from? Is the task boring or too challenging? Are you afraid of making a mistake or do you consider the task to be too risky for you? These are the questions you need to ask yourself when you are trying to break the cycle. If you still can't figure it out, then self-reflection is necessary to identify the underlying cause of your procrastination.

THE UNDERLYING CAUSES OF PROCRASTINATION

There are multiple causes of procrastination and many of them are rooted in psychology. They are sometimes hidden deep in our past but are triggered by certain emotions or events that bring about the aversion to carrying out a specific task. Here are some of the main underlying causes of procrastination:

Lack of Self-Regulation

Self-regulation is the ability to control our behaviors and impulses. Without effective self-regulation, we're prone to giving in to immediate desires at the expense of our long-term goals. This means that we prioritize the things that give us immediate satisfaction over what is truly good for us. For example, we could be easily distracted by cute cat videos because they provide feelings of happiness and joy instead of completing a project that has the ability to improve our position at work. When we start working on the project, we experience discomfort or even unhappiness, which then gives us an urge to start watching videos again to feel better. Giving in to that urge means that we lack self-regulation.

Temporal Discounting

Temporal discounting is a term in psychology that refers to the decrease in the value of something because the reward is not immediate. Therefore, procrastinators tend to think that achieving their goals is so far away that it is not important right now. There are other activities and tasks that can provide them with immediate gratification and these, therefore, seem more valuable compared to those whose rewards we will reap in the distant future. Academic procrastination is a good example of this.

Self-Esteem Issues

Additionally, procrastination can also be linked to self-esteem issues. When we believe that our worth is tied to our achievements, we might procrastinate to avoid potential failure and protect our self-esteem. If we never complete a difficult task, we can't fail at it. Our thoughts tell us that this is a good defensive move when in fact, we are sabotaging ourselves as we keep putting a limit on what we can do.

Fear of Failure

Fear is a powerful emotion, and it can hinder us from growing by keeping us in our comfort zone. When we are faced with a task or opportunity that is beyond our comfort zone, we are afraid that it might lead to failure. This leads us to delay or avoid it altogether. When we're afraid of failing, the safest option often seems to be not to try at all. We associate failure with shame, embarrassment, and inadequacy when, in reality, it is a normal part of life. However, procrastination itself is a form of failure. It prevents us from reaching our potential and accomplishing our goals.

Perfectionism

Perfectionism and procrastination are closely linked. Perfectionists set high standards for themselves, and the fear of not meeting those standards can lead to procrastination. If a task can't be completed perfectly, a perfectionist might prefer not to start it at all. There can be many reasons for not starting, such as not having all the information, still contemplating the best approach, and waiting for inspiration to strike. However, while it's good to strive for excellence, the all-or-nothing thinking of perfectionism can be counterproductive. It can make us fear mistakes and view any flaw as a sign of failure which, in turn, feeds into our fear of failure, strengthening the urge to procrastinate.

Lack of Challenge or Boredom

Boredom and lack of challenge can significantly contribute to procrastination. When you are not motivated by or have any interest in the tasks you have, they are more likely to be postponed in favor of activities that provide immediate gratification. Likewise, when there is no challenge involved, you won't see the need to complete the task timeously, believing that it is well within your skillset to breeze through. However, this can be a dangerous practice as you lose precious time and may end up missing out on something important or making silly mistakes due to your nonchalance. This is something students are familiar with when they fail to study because they believe they already have a firm grip on the content being tested in an exam.

Underlying Illness

Underlying illnesses, particularly mental health disorders, can significantly contribute to procrastination. Conditions like depression, anxiety disorders, ADHD (attention deficit hyperactivity disorder), and chronic stress are closely linked with procrastination. Depression, characterized by feelings of sadness, lack of energy, and loss of interest, can make even routine tasks appear daunting, leading to procrastination (Boyes, 2019). Similarly, individuals with anxiety disorders might procrastinate as a coping mechanism to avoid the anticipated stress associated with certain tasks.

ADHD is also closely associated with procrastination. A key feature of ADHD is difficulties with executive function, including problems with self-regulation, organizing, and prioritizing tasks (Niermann & Scheres, 2014). These cognitive challenges can make it harder to start and complete tasks, leading to procrastination. More importantly, these illnesses do not just lead to procrastination—the relationship can also be bidirectional. For example, the anxiety caused by procrastination can further exacerbate mental health conditions, creating a vicious cycle.

Poor Time Management

If an individual has poor time management, it will feed the procrastination cycle when tasks pile up, deadlines are missed, and stress levels rise. When you experience these effects, it will make you procrastinate more because the task now brings about a sense of dread. One particular aspect of poor time management is the failure to prioritize tasks effectively. If individuals do not prioritize their tasks based on urgency and importance, they may find themselves overwhelmed by the sheer volume of work, leading to decision paralysis and subsequent procrastination. In addition, a lack of a structured routine or schedule can also foster procrastination. Without a clear plan, individuals may feel directionless and find it easy to defer tasks in favor of more immediate or enjoyable activities.

TRIGGERS AND PATTERNS THAT LEAD TO PROCRASTINATION

The last thing you need to know about procrastination before working toward overcoming it is the triggers and patterns that give rise to procrastination. Most people have a combination of internal and external triggers and patterns that cause them to delay tasks. When you learn to recognize them, you are one step closer to working to overcome them.

Internal Triggers

Internal triggers mostly consist of our emotions and thoughts. We have already gone through quite a few of them in the previous sections. Negative emotions, such as boredom, anxiety, or feeling overwhelmed, often trigger procrastination as an avoidance strategy. Thus, if you find yourself delaying a task, try to evaluate which of these emotions are triggering your procrastination. This will lead to a better understanding of your procrastination and your emotions.

External Triggers

External triggers of procrastination usually deal with our environments. An environment that offers multiple distractions, such as a noisy workplace or a cluttered study area, can easily take attention away from the task at hand. Similarly, constant access to smartphones and the internet can serve as a continuous source of diversion, leading to procrastination. This is something we are all familiar with as our devices are usually a major source of distraction and problems in multiple areas of our lives.

Common Patterns of Procrastination

When you begin to pay more attention to your procrastination, you might begin to recognize common or recurring patterns that give rise to it. There are three main elements to focus on here: time, tasks, and feelings. The first pattern is based on time. Some people may find that they tend to procrastinate more at certain times of the day, month, or year. For example, the afternoon slump a few hours before you leave work can make you feel as if you don't really want to start on a new task, so you delay it until the next day. Similarly, some people find that the weeks before Christmas or before they go on vacation are not the best time to work.

The second pattern is based on the task. Certain tasks are considered too challenging, too boring, or the deadline is too far away for people to be concerned about. Thus, they will find reasons to avoid the task such as there is more important work to get done. This may be disguised as prioritization, but it is actually working on tasks that they find more attractive or rewarding.

The last pattern is based on emotions. When certain emotions like anxiety, fear, or even sadness arise, people may procrastinate as a defensive coping mechanism. They don't want to experience the emotion any further, so they avoid the task. These three patterns are what you need to be able to recognize procrastination in your life and be able to get a better understanding of the root cause. In all honesty, there could be several causes, triggers, and patterns involved in your procrastination—that is not an unusual occurrence. The important thing is that you have knowledge of them and you can now begin working on eliminating your procrastination.

CHAPTER 3

OVERCOMING PROCRASTINATION —A MINDSET SHIFT

Beginning your journey to overcome procrastination requires a mindset shift. As we have learned in the previous chapters, procrastination originates from the thoughts and emotions that run through our minds when faced with a task. Therefore, changing our mindsets to one that is proactive instead of reactive, is crucial to overcoming procrastination. A mindset shift always takes time because it involves breaking habits and thought patterns that you have developed throughout your life. However, it is not impossible—it just requires consistency and commitment. This chapter will help you shift your mindset and develop strategies to maintain this change.

CULTIVATING A PROACTIVE MINDSET TOWARD TASKS

When people hear the word *proactive*, they immediately think of taking action. However, a proactive mindset is not just about jumping into action, but also considering the implications of your actions. This involves identifying potential problems, planning ahead, and making informed decisions. It also requires resilience and adaptability, as you'll often face unexpected challenges with tasks. Thus, instead of procrastinating when faced with a task, you immediately start breaking down your task and finding the best ways to accomplish it instead of delaying it.

The first step toward cultivating a proactive mindset is recognizing that procrastination is not a character flaw but a habit that can be broken. It is about unlearning old patterns and training your brain to respond differently to tasks. You need to think about work differently, viewing tasks not as burdens but as opportunities for growth and learning. No matter the outcome, the task will provide a lesson and give you the opportunity to improve yourself. Like with any bad habit, procrastination becomes an automatic response. Therefore, you have to consciously make an effort to pause and analyze a task without the cognitive biases you have developed taking over.

Secondly, you need to approach tasks with curiosity instead of dread. Try to figure out what you can learn from it or how it contributes to your growth, as this will give you a different perspective of the task. This shift in perspective will make your tasks seem less intimidating and more inviting. Therefore, instead of your brain immediately trying to avoid a challenging task, it will take time to consider what the task entails and how you can benefit from it. This ensures that you begin to think about tasks differently and eliminate the dread from ever occurring.

Thirdly, you should practice mindful task engagement. Be present in the task, focusing not on the anxiety of the outcome, but on the process. With full engagement and attention, tasks become less overwhelming. Furthermore, if you focus on the process and break it down into smaller parts, it becomes more manageable. Lastly, being proactive means taking responsibility for your time and actions. Prioritize your tasks, setting boundaries to protect your time and energy. Recognize that every moment spent on a task is a choice, and make those choices count.

SETTING CLEAR, SPECIFIC, AND MOTIVATING GOALS

One of the best catalysts for overcoming procrastination is setting clear, specific, and motivating goals. In doing so, your tasks become manageable pieces that have a clear timeline and provide a clear direction for action. Furthermore, as you complete each portion of the task, you will be motivated to continue as you can monitor your progress clearly.

In order to do this, you need to first define your goals. They should be specific enough to give a clear path but flexible enough to allow for adjustments along the way. We all know that things never go smoothly all the time, so we need to be prepared to adapt when needed. Thus, your goals must be clear and specific, but you must not be limited by them. For example, instead of aiming to read every night before going to bed, you could aim to read five pages every day. In this way, you can still read every night, but you can also aim to fit this in at any time of the day if you know you are going out with friends. Once your goals are defined, break them down into smaller, manageable tasks. Each task should be a step toward achieving the goal, turning a daunting task into achievable steps. The satisfaction derived from completing these tasks will motivate you to continue. You will also begin to realize that the goal was not that daunting and just needed a clear plan of action.

The goals you define should not only be clear and specific, but they should also be motivating. You can gain so much inspiration and motivation by allowing your goals to align with your values and passions, giving you a personal stake in their achievement. This alignment intensifies your motivation, driving you to overcome procrastination. The last thing you should aim for when it comes to setting goals is to hold yourself accountable. This might involve telling a friend about your goals or making a public commitment. Accountability provides an additional layer of motivation, prompting you to act rather than procrastinate. If you don't act, people will know that you are not sticking to your goals and this will spur you into action.

HARNESSING MOTIVATION AND FINDING A SENSE OF PURPOSE

Following changing your mindset and setting goals, finding a sense of purpose in your work can help you overcome procrastination. If we don't see the value in what we're doing, it's easy to put it off because it's not that important to us. However, when we find our motivation and purpose, tasks become engaging and worthwhile because they mean something to us. This sense of purpose should even drive your mindset shift and help clarify your goals to a point where your path ahead is clear and unfaltering.

To do this, you need to first answer a simple question: "Why?" Why are you doing what you are doing? Why is your goal important to you? The answers to these questions will identify your sense of purpose. For example, the earlier defined goal of reading five pages every day—are you doing it to expand your knowledge? To enhance your career? Or maybe you are doing it to teach your child how to read. Whatever the case may be, it is your purpose and it should motivate you and spark activity rather than procrastination.

Next, you need to utilize intrinsic motivation as opposed to extrinsic motivation. Intrinsic motivation comes from within, while extrinsic motivation is driven by external rewards or punishments. It is easy to push extrinsic motivation aside or delay it because you are still in control of when it occurs. Intrinsic motivation, however, is immediate and can be a powerful way to bring about action. No one wants to miss out on the glorious feeling of achieving goals that are important to them. This is why we might as well use it to our advantage.

When you have your sense of purpose, you then need to cultivate a growth mindset. A growth mindset embraces challenges as opportunities for learning and development, fueling your motivation to engage in tasks. There is no such thing as failure when you have a growth mindset as every outcome, whether positive or negative, provides a valuable lesson. Combining these factors, alongside defining long-term goals important to you, will definitely help you work toward the vision you have of your life.

EMBRACING DISCIPLINE AND SELF-CONTROL AS HABITS

Remember how we said that overcoming procrastination takes commitment and consistency? Well, discipline is all about consistency. It's about showing up and doing the work, whether you feel like it or not. It's built over time, by consistently choosing to work on your tasks instead of putting them off. Discipline is what drives people who we admire for their good habits. Self-control, on the other hand, is about managing your impulses. It's about choosing the important over the immediate gratification, the productive over the pleasurable. It's about recognizing your distractions and resisting them. If you make it your mission to build these two habits, you will make yourself an unstoppable force.

Building these habits takes time and practice. Therefore, it requires commitment and an understanding of what is good for you. Like with any goal, you should start small, with simple, achievable tasks. Think of your discipline and self-control as muscles that you need to work on. The stronger these muscles get, the more complex tasks you can take on. To make this easier, you should also aim to develop routines that support your discipline. For example, you can design your environment to minimize distractions and make it easy for you to get started on your tasks.

Remember, overcoming procrastination is not a one-time event, but a process. It's about continuously shifting your mindset, setting motivating goals, harnessing your motivation, and cultivating discipline and self-control. It's a journey of personal growth and development, with each step taking you closer to your full potential.

CHAPTER 4

EFFECTIVE STRATEGIES TO STOP PROCRASTINATING

The next step to overcoming procrastination is to start adopting effective strategies that will help you along the way. Since procrastination is essentially an issue of mismanaged priorities and time, we need to find strategies that will help us with this. In this chapter, we will look at some of the best ways to effectively use our time, avoid distractions, and ensure that we prioritize our work correctly.

PRIORITIZATION AND EFFECTIVE TIME MANAGEMENT

Time management and prioritization go hand in hand. If you don't know how to prioritize your work properly, you can't expect to be using your time properly. Devoting time to unnecessary tasks when there are others that require urgent attention is also a form of unintentional procrastination. This is why it is of the utmost importance that you learn to prioritize correctly in order to ensure that your time is well spent. The best way to do this is to make use of an Eisenhower Decision Matrix. This matrix has an interesting origin, having been inspired by a quote from an American general named Dwight. D Eisenhower (Dorin, 2022).

It basically entails splitting your tasks up into four categories:

- those that are urgent and important
- those that are urgent and not important
- those that are not urgent but important
- those that are not urgent and not important

You will need to go through your list of tasks and then categorize them into the quadrants of the decision matrix. This will provide a clear picture of what needs immediate attention, what can be scheduled for later, what can be delegated, and what can be eliminated. If you can do this on a regular basis, your tasks will be prioritized accurately.

To ensure that you manage your time effectively, you have to assess how you work. Some people are more productive in the mornings and choose to do their most important tasks then, while others take a longer time to settle into work and prefer to work on important tasks later in the day. Additionally, time management techniques can be very effective and ensure a balanced day.

TIME MANAGEMENT TECHNIQUES

There are several time management techniques that you can use to ensure that your time is used effectively. However, two techniques are simple and guarantee efficacy: time-blocking and making use of task lists and planners.

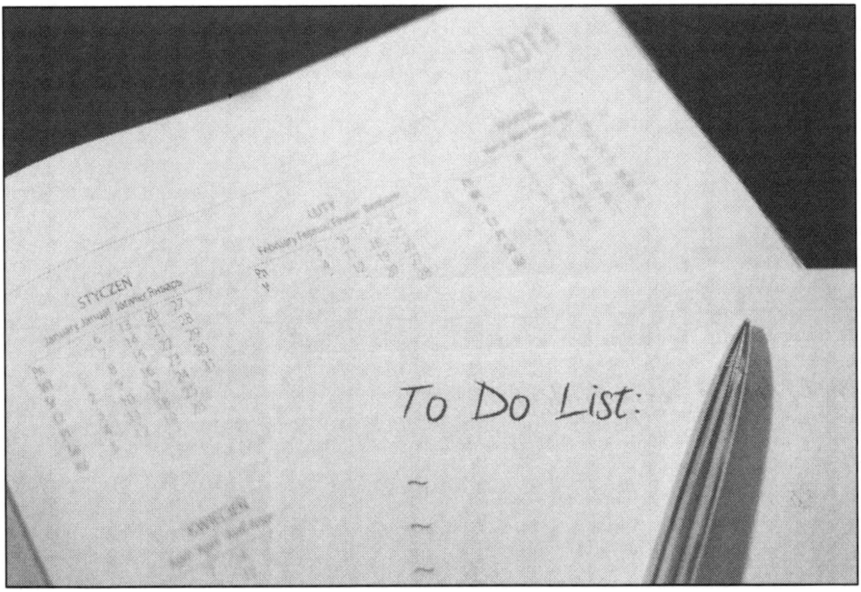

Time-Blocking

Time-blocking involves dividing your day into dedicated blocks of time for specific tasks or activities. By assigning specific time slots to tasks, you create a structured framework that helps you stay focused and accountable. Here's how you can effectively utilize time-blocking to boost productivity and conquer procrastination:

1. **Start by identifying your most important and urgent tasks.** These could be work-related projects, personal goals, or even routine activities. Once you have a clear understanding of your priorities, allocate specific time blocks for each task in your schedule. Ensure that you set realistic and attainable goals for each time block, considering your energy levels and the complexity of the task at hand. Remember to include breaks in your schedule to recharge and maintain productivity throughout the day. You should also always aim to set realistic time blocks. The aim of time

blocks is not to make you do more in less time but to ensure that you stick to your tasks in the allocated slot, thereby maintaining momentum and leaving less room for procrastination.

2. **Establish a routine and stick to it.** Consistency is key when it comes to time-blocking. Train yourself to follow the designated time blocks diligently, resisting the urge to deviate or procrastinate. Treat these blocks as sacred appointments with yourself and avoid distractions during these periods. By developing a habit of adhering to your schedule, you create a sense of discipline that aids in combating procrastination. Remember the schedule is there to help you but you must also be dedicated to making it work!
3. **Regularly review and evaluate your time-blocking strategy.** Assess whether you were able to complete tasks within the allocated time frames and make adjustments as needed. Be flexible and open to modifying your schedule to accommodate unexpected events or new priorities. By continuously refining your time-blocking technique, you can optimize your time usage and gradually minimize the tendency to procrastinate. In addition, the better you get at adhering to your schedule, the more confidence you will gain in your ability to complete tasks within timeframes. This will enable you to set deadlines better and give better estimates to others regarding work deadlines.

Effectively Using Task Lists and Planners

We must first be clear: Time-blocking and task lists and planners are two different things. They both achieve the same goal of helping you manage your time better and are invaluable tools for combating procrastination and staying organized. However, their approaches are different. Task lists and planners provide a visual representation of your tasks and help you prioritize and manage your workload effectively. To make the most of task lists and planners, consider the following strategies:

1. **Create a comprehensive and actionable task list.** Write down all the tasks that need to be accomplished, breaking them down into smaller, more manageable subtasks. This helps to prevent you from becoming overwhelmed and gives you a clear roadmap of what needs to be done. Prioritize your tasks based on urgency and importance using the Eisenhower Matrix, and consider assigning deadlines to create a sense of accountability.

2. **Explore different formats for task lists and planners.** You will need to look around to find what works best for you. Some individuals prefer the traditional pen-and-paper approach, while others opt for digital tools or apps. Experiment with different systems until you find one that aligns with your preferences and enhances your productivity. Some people prefer simple calendar views, while others prefer more elaborate color-coded task views. The key is to find a method that you enjoy using and that makes it easy for you to track and update your tasks.

3. **Break down your tasks into manageable chunks and assign realistic timelines.** This not only helps to avoid unnecessary stress and high-pressure situations but also provides a sense of progress and accomplishment as you complete each subtask. Celebrating these small victories can motivate you to continue working and reduce the likelihood of procrastination.

4. **Regularly review and update your task list and planner.** Take a few minutes at the beginning or end of each day to assess your progress and make adjustments as needed. Reflect on your productivity levels and identify any recurring patterns of procrastination. By consistently evaluating and refining your task management system, you can fine-tune your approach and boost your overall efficiency.

Using these prioritization and time management strategies in combination ensures that you use your time in the best way. It also promotes productivity by eliminating unnecessary tasks that will take valuable time. The more you put this into practice, the easier it will become over time.

CREATE AN OPTIMAL WORK ENVIRONMENT FOR PRODUCTIVITY

To decrease procrastination further and maximize productivity, you can work on creating the optimal work environment. This entails you working to eliminate distractions and surrounding yourself with people and objects that keep you focused and productive in everything that you do. It is important to note, however, that an optimal work environment will look different for different people. For example, some may need complete silence to work uninterrupted, while others need some kind of background noise because silence can lead to wandering thoughts. Thus, you need to gain a better understanding of yourself and what type of environment can maximize your productivity while minimizing procrastination.

To do this, you need to start paying attention to how you work currently and what works for you and what doesn't. The noise level, as mentioned above, is a good example. You should also pay attention to factors such as lighting, temperature, and comfort. Natural light and a comfortable temperature are generally preferable to most people. This ensures that you are comfortable and not straining your eyes or wishing for a jacket while you work. In addition, the workspace should be clean, organized, and free from clutter. A cluttered workspace can lead to a cluttered mind, causing anxiety and hindering productivity. Also, if your workspace is clutter-free, you save time by not having to rummage through everything to find what you need for a specific task.

Lastly, there's nothing wrong with personalizing your workspace. In fact, a personalized workspace can stimulate creativity and reduce stress. When you surround yourself with things that are important to you such as plants, photos, or artwork, it makes you feel more at peace when you work.

Furthermore, you can have encouraging quotes or photos of your kids that will motivate you to do your best at work and stay focused on what is important. It is also worth noting that an optimal workspace is also applicable to individuals that work from home. Being in a place of comfort does not automatically mean that you have the best space to work. In fact, working from home presents its own set of challenges and distractions that you have to address. Something as simple as sitting in front of a window can take away time from your work as you pay attention to the cars driving down the street. Thus, it is crucial that you assess your current working tendencies to create the optimal work environment.

ADDRESSING DISTRACTIONS AND TEMPTATIONS THAT HINDER WORK

Distractions these days come in all forms. Colleagues, family members, phones, emails, text messages, social media, and even the internet in general can be hugely distracting. It can also leave you feeling horribly overwhelmed when you try to address everything. This is one of the main reasons that we feel that there is never enough time—our attention is drawn everywhere else. Therefore, to keep your focus on your tasks, you have to ensure that you eliminate distractions and get rid of temptations that draw your attention away.

To do this, you have to first identify the distractions and temptations that are most likely to hinder your work. Is it social media? Your phone? Is it your noisy coworkers? Sometimes, distractions can even fool you into thinking you are working. For example, a quick email to your boss may lead to you spending 30 minutes checking your inbox, or a colleague stopping by to ask a question could turn into an hour-long chat about their upcoming vacation. Identifying these elements may take time, and may even require making a note every time you lose focus while you work. However, once you know what they are, you can take active steps to limit or eliminate them.

This could mean implementing things such as setting specific times for checking emails or social media, using noise-canceling headphones, or communicating your work hours to those around you to avoid unnecessary interruptions. You can even delete apps you find distracting from your phone, which will reduce the chances of you using your other devices to access them. Even the simple act of closing your office door can help you stay focused on your tasks and reduce procrastination.

UTILIZING TECHNOLOGICAL TOOLS TO OVERCOME PROCRASTINATION

When used appropriately, technology can be a powerful ally against procrastination. There are numerous apps and tools available that can help manage time effectively, prioritize tasks, break tasks into manageable steps, create a productive work environment, and limit distractions. This decreases the amount of time you have to spend planning and prioritizing your work. Let's take a look at the type of tools now available that you can use to effectively overcome procrastination.

Time Management Tools

Managing your time is more than just having a good daily planner. There are currently many tools and resources available that can help you manage your time better. Firstly, there are time management tools that can track how much time you spend on projects and even on distractions. This gives you an idea of where most of your time goes, when you are most productive, and how you can optimize your time better. Secondly, there are tools that will help you stick to your schedule better by providing reminders and alarms when you need to start on another task or when it is time for a break. You want to eliminate procrastination and boost productivity, but you must also remember to maintain a healthy work/life balance.

Task Management Tools

These tools have become extremely popular in recent years. Task management tools are effective for organizing your work, setting priorities, and tracking your progress. It is now possible to create individual tasks, assign them to different categories or projects, set deadlines, and add subtasks. They keep all your tasks neatly organized and also keep your mind clutter-free from having to remember specific details. You can even use these tools to store files relevant to a task, which means that everything is in one place and you don't have to search for them. By utilizing time management tools, you can easily track your progress and this can even provide a motivational boost when you assess your productivity.

Distraction-Blocking Tools

Yes, there are even apps that can help you deal with distractions. These tools work to block apps that distract you while you work for a specific amount of time. For example, you can block your social media apps while you are at work during the day and they will be active once again in the evenings. They will work on whichever apps or web pages you assign them to and can be extremely effective in blocking distractions from your electronic devices.

Motivational Tools

There are several motivational tools also available that can help you track your goals and motivate you to achieve them. They provide a visual representation that can be more motivating than text and they also have clever ways to keep you working toward your goals. For example, certain tools work to turn your goals into a game, with your progress resulting in you completing more levels and earning rewards in the game. Thus, every task you complete contributes to your "leveling up" in the game.

Mindfulness Tools

Finally, mindfulness and relaxation apps can aid in dealing with stress and anxiety, which often contribute to procrastination. They offer guided meditations, calming music, and other features that can help clear your mind, refocus, and approach your tasks with a calm and centered mindset.

Remember, the fight against procrastination is a continuous one. It requires conscious effort, practice, and self-reflection. With these strategies and a determined mindset, it is possible to conquer procrastination and elevate productivity to new heights.

CHAPTER 5
OVERCOMING MENTAL BARRIERS AND LIMITING BELIEFS

To implement strategies to overcome procrastination, there is one more area that you need to work on to make it effective: your brain. Procrastination is often rooted in limiting beliefs, which create mental barriers that stop us from acting when we should. It is one of the internal triggers that we discussed earlier and you need to be able to understand, recognize, and free yourself from them to strengthen your ability to overcome procrastination.

IDENTIFYING AND DEBUNKING LIMITING BELIEFS THAT FOSTER PROCRASTINATION

In order to deal with limiting beliefs, you have to first know what they are. They are the thoughts that limit your activity by telling you things like *I am not smart enough*, *I am not good at this task*, or *I always fail.* It makes you procrastinate by leading you to believe that you are not capable of achieving the task. Identifying these beliefs is of the utmost importance. A practical way to identify limiting beliefs is through self-reflection and introspection.

Monitor your thought patterns, especially when faced with tasks that you tend to procrastinate on. It is also helpful to keep a journal of your thoughts, feelings, and actions. This can help you spot patterns or recurring thoughts that indicate the presence of limiting beliefs. Regularly reviewing and analyzing your journal entries can bring clarity and help you identify these subconscious barriers.

Once you have these thoughts identified, you can then start to debunk these beliefs. This entails questioning their validity. Are they objectively true, or are they based on past experiences, assumptions, or fears? Often, limiting beliefs stem from past failures or situations that provided negative feedback, but they don't accurately reflect our abilities or potential. More often than not, you'll find these beliefs lack substantial evidence. The more you ask questions that challenge these thoughts, the easier it is to realize just how untrue they are. You also might find it helpful to list instances when you successfully completed similar tasks or faced challenges effectively. This can help you realize that your belief isn't an accurate reflection of your capabilities.

You can also work on replacing these negative thoughts with positive affirmations that boost your self-esteem and confidence. Instead of telling yourself "I can't do this task," you could say, "I can learn to do this task" or "I can seek help to accomplish this task." This subtle shift in language can have a profound impact on your mindset, helping you transition from a state of self-doubt to a state of positivity, possibility, and action.

OVERCOMING FEAR AND SELF-DOUBT THAT BLOCK ACTION

Procrastination is often fueled by fear and self-doubt. Fear of failure, fear of success, and even fear of judgment can trigger a paralysis that keeps us from taking action or making a decision. Alongside these fears, self-doubt further exacerbates procrastination, making us question our abilities and worthiness. Overcoming these barriers is a vital part of defeating procrastination and unlocking productivity. To overcome fear and self-doubt, we must first know what they are and how they affect us.

Fear, in the context of procrastination, typically revolves around the potential negative outcomes of an action. The fear of failure might lead us to think, "What if I can't do it?" On the flip side, the fear of success could bring thoughts like, "What if I can't handle the responsibilities that come with success?" The fear of judgment may cause worry about the opinions of others, prompting thoughts such as, "What will people think if I fail?" Self-doubt is the inner voice that questions our abilities and potential. It makes us underestimate ourselves and magnifies our perceived shortcomings, resulting in thoughts like, "I'm not good enough" or "I don't have what it takes." Both fear and self-doubt generate limiting beliefs and must be dealt with accordingly.

To overcome fear, you must first acknowledge its presence. Fear is often so deeply hidden in our subconscious minds that it does take a while to find it. Once you do, it is best to re-identify your fear as a guide rather than a barrier. Fear is a natural response designed to keep us safe, but it can be overly protective, keeping us from growth and achievement. Try to see your fear as a signpost that indicates areas where you need to grow and learn rather than as a red light that stops progress. You can also try imagining the worst-case scenario and trying to work out how you will handle it. By doing this, you begin to feel like you can take on a task without fearing what would happen because you have already dealt with the worst-case scenario in your mind.

To conquer self-doubt, you must reaffirm your belief in your ability to succeed. This can be achieved by acknowledging your accomplishments, however small they may seem. Make a list of things you have achieved, skills you have, or challenges you've overcome. You will be surprised at how extensive this list can be and whenever self-doubt creeps in, you can review it and remember that you can achieve what you set your mind to. At the end of the day, you must remember that fear and self-doubt are natural feelings. Every single person on the planet experiences these emotions and the only thing that sets them apart is whether they let it rule their actions, or whether they learn to deal with them.

CULTIVATING A GROWTH MINDSET AND CONFIDENCE IN YOUR ABILITIES

A growth mindset, as proposed by psychologist Carol Dweck, refers to the belief that our basic skills and abilities can be developed and improved through dedication and hard work (*Carol Dweck: A Summary of the Two Mindsets*, 2015). To have a growth mindset, you must exhibit resilience, must not be afraid of taking risks, and you need to see failure as an opportunity to learn and grow. Cultivating a growth mindset begins with understanding that your intelligence and talent are not fixed and are just starting points of your true potential. With effort, strategy, and input from others, we can grow, learn, and improve.

One key aspect of a growth mindset is viewing challenges as opportunities. When you encounter a daunting task, instead of avoiding it (and procrastinating), see it as an opportunity to learn something new or improve your skills. Embracing failure as a part of learning is another essential component of a growth mindset. Failures and setbacks are not dead-ends but are stepping stones on the path to success. Each mistake you make is a lesson that brings you one step closer to your goal. By developing a growth mindset, you are acknowledging that learning never ends. If you see every task and challenge as a learning experience, there is never any need to procrastinate as every action will provide a lesson no matter the outcome.

Then, there's confidence. Confidence in one's abilities comes with time and experience. You have to hype yourself up every now and then! Think about how far you have come and how much you have accomplished. That is no fluke—it is a result of your hard work and talents. Furthermore, when working toward your goals, each milestone you achieve should be boosting your confidence. Cultivating a growth mindset and confidence in your abilities is a lifelong journey. It requires patience, effort, and the courage to face challenges, make mistakes, and learn from them. But the rewards are definitely worth it. With a growth mindset and strong self-confidence, you'll find that tasks become less intimidating, and the urge to procrastinate will be drastically reduced.

BUILDING RESILIENCE TO FACE CHALLENGES AND STAY MOTIVATED

Resilience is the ability to recover from setbacks and challenges. To have resilience means that you will continue trying until you succeed, trying different approaches as you learn more from each attempt. Thus, if you have resilience, you do not fear challenges or failure because you know that no matter what, you will persevere. This simple knowledge can immensely reduce procrastination brought on by mental barriers. Resilience involves maintaining a positive mindset, staying focused on long-term goals, and having the determination to keep moving forward, even in the face of setbacks. To build resilience, you need to embrace challenges and adopt a growth mindset, which we have been through already. You also need to practice self-care, have a good support system, and work on your problem-solving skills and your willingness to persevere.

Taking care of your physical and mental well-being is crucial for building resilience. This is something that is needed to ensure that you have the energy and mental clarity to face challenges with resilience. If you neglect your self-care, you will be struggling with mental fatigue and physical tiredness that will make it impossible to remain positive and focused on your tasks. A supportive network of friends, family, or mentors who can provide guidance, encouragement, and a listening ear is also beneficial if you want to build resilience. They can help you remember your abilities when you are struggling and remind you that you can get through your tasks with perseverance.

Lastly, problem-solving skills can also help you build resilience. If you have good problem-solving skills, you remain calm in challenges and analyze the best way to approach it. You can strengthen your problem-solving skills by practicing creative thinking, brainstorming alternative approaches, and seeking out different perspectives. Embracing a mindset of resourcefulness and adaptability, and knowing that there are multiple ways to overcome challenges, can be a great asset in any situation and helps you eliminate all mental barriers that tell you that you cannot do something.

By working on all these elements collectively, you can get rid of every thought that tells you "I can't." It instead cultivates the mindset that "I can't, yet—but I will." If you continue to put these strategies into action every day, even for a little while, you contribute to a more productive future.

CHAPTER 6

PROCRASTINATION AS A FORM OF SELF-SABOTAGE

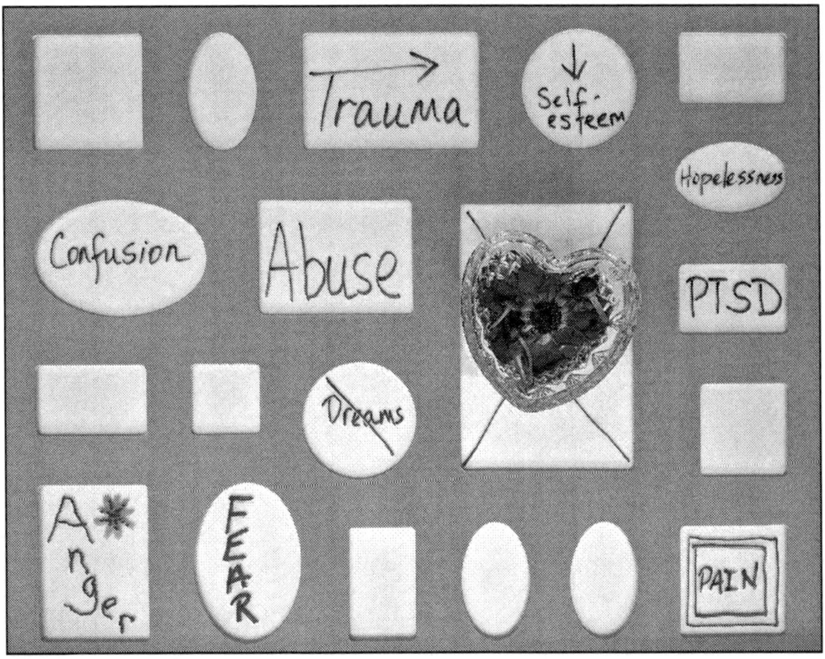

Self-sabotage is not something we talk about often. After all, why would we deliberately cause problems for ourselves when we really want to achieve our goals? However, the truth is that many people might not even know that they are self-sabotaging with their daily behaviors—and this can severely hinder your chances of progressing in life. Procrastination is actually one of the most common forms of self-sabotage. The fact that you delay your tasks means that you are delaying yourself from achieving your goals. In this chapter, we will discuss whether you are self-sabotaging by procrastinating, how you can identify it, and what you can do to overcome it.

UNDERSTANDING PROCRASTINATION AS A FORM OF SELF-SABOTAGE

Self-sabotage in itself is any behavior by an individual that prevents them from achieving their goals. The reasons why a person self-sabotages vary from past trauma to coping mechanisms that they have developed unknowingly. To understand why you self-sabotage, you need to delve deep into your past and look for the origins of your self-sabotaging behavior. Of course, to do this, you need to first be able to identify your self-sabotaging thoughts and behaviors.

If you are self-sabotaging, these are some of the signs that you need to look out for.

1. Avoidance

If you often find yourself avoiding people and situations that make you uncomfortable, you are staying within your comfort zone. This prevents any meaningful growth that occurs when you learn from challenging situations. Also, if you avoid what makes you uncomfortable, you will never learn to see things from different perspectives.

2. Aiming Too Low

If you find yourself always having small long-term goals that are easily achievable, you are self-sabotaging. Yes, large goals can be broken down into smaller, easier attainable tasks; but you should always have goals that challenge you and aim to make you the person you want to be. Continuously playing it safe means that you stop yourself from being the best possible version of yourself.

3. Creating Conflict

Another common sign of self-sabotage is if you often find yourself arguing with colleagues, friends, family, and partners. Procrastinating instead of dealing with issues in your relationships could be a way of sabotaging them. Do you not feel worthy of the relationship? Are you always thinking about how much better they are than you? These are clear signs of self-sabotage.

4. Having Control

Many people seek control of situations—and people—in an attempt to feel like they are being proactive. However, it could also just be another way of introducing conflict, or delay in situations. It becomes very easy to quit or find an excuse as to why a situation is not going according to your plan. You also fail to realize that the only person you are hurting is yourself.

5. Seeking Approval

When we constantly seek the approval of others, it means that we don't approve of ourselves and need external validation. This can be a form of self-sabotage because if we constantly seek approval but never get it, we think of it as confirmation of not being good enough. In turn, it leads to reinforced negative thoughts that can prevent us from acting on our everyday tasks.

6. Excuses

Do you find yourself often making excuses as to why you can't do something? This is classic procrastination, but it can also be self-sabotaging behavior if these excuses are holding you back from personal and professional progress.

7. Comparisons

Constantly comparing yourself to others or using them as a yardstick for your success is also a form of self-sabotage. This is because if you always compare yourself to others, you are not actually tracking your own progress and you are ignoring your personal growth. When you fail to self-evaluate and use others as comparisons, you stop yourself from taking action by believing that you are not good enough.

8. Taking Unnecessary Risks

Engaging in risky behaviors is a classic form of self-sabotage. People indulge in alcohol, food, drugs, and sex as a form of gratification while avoiding important events in their lives. Procrastinating by carrying out these behaviors instead of doing things that will ensure your improvement will only make you more miserable and take you further away from your goals.

If any of these sound familiar, you may be self-sabotaging yourself without knowing. These are all possible ways in which you procrastinate as well because it all brings about a delay in action. Thus, if you are procrastinating as a way to self-sabotage, you need to start working on getting rid of these behaviors by finding their source. Work backward to try to find out when they began and if there were specific events that brought them on. In this way, you can begin to identify if your self-sabotaging is a result of fear, anxiety, or self-doubt.

ADDRESSING FEAR AND SELF-SABOTAGE ASSOCIATED WITH PROCRASTINATION

Fear plays a significant role in self-sabotaging procrastination. Fear of failure, judgment, or uncertainty can prevent individuals from taking action. This is why it is important to work to overcome this fear. Fear is a hard emotion to deal with as it is so deeply rooted in past events. The best way to handle fear is to work to reframe the way we perceive failure and uncertainty. This is because most of our fear comes from past failures and what occurred after it—how we felt after we failed, what others thought of us, and questioning our ability to ever succeed. However, instead of viewing failures as signs of weakness or inadequacy, they should be seen as opportunities for growth and learning.

This is where adopting a growth mindset can come in handy. If you change the way you perceive failure, you can deal with the fear that leads to self-sabotaging procrastination. If you see failures as opportunities for growth and learning, there is nothing to fear. You will not fear failure because you will know that failure will bring a lesson with it that will help you improve. You will not fear what others think of your failure, because you will show them that it was just a stepping stone to success. If they still judge you for it, it is only because they themselves do not have a growth mindset. And lastly, you will not fear not being able to ever succeed because each new attempt brings you closer to your goal as you improve your approach every time. Therefore, a growth mindset is a powerful tool to combat fear.

Self-reflection is also crucial for overcoming the fear that causes individuals to self-sabotage. This is because only when you reflect on your past will you be able to identify the events that served as catalysts for your fear. You can then assess how you used to work before the event and whether your self-sabotaging procrastination has impacted the way you work and obtain results after. Has your overall performance been impacted? Do you think you would be further in your career by now if you had not started procrastinating? How many other ways are you self-sabotaging other than procrastination?

PRACTICAL TOOLS AND TACTICS FOR OVERCOMING SELF-SABOTAGING PROCRASTINATION

To overcome procrastination that has risen from self-sabotage, you have to be willing to put in some effort. Along with the usual techniques to overcome procrastination, there are a few extra steps that you need to take to handle your self-sabotaging. As discussed earlier, you need to find the source of your behaviors—how they came about and how they have impacted your progress over the years. Then you need to adopt a growth mindset to deal with the fear of failure, which is a major cause of self-sabotaging procrastination. Along with these two techniques, you can also try these:

Mindfulness

When you are mindful of your thoughts and behaviors, you can nip them in the bud if they do not serve you. If you are working on a task and self-sabotaging thoughts start creeping in that start lowering your self-esteem, you need to stop and question their validity. Where are they coming from? Are they helping you or hurting your progress? If you are mindful of everything that you do, you can catch these thoughts before they have a chance to affect you.

Small Steps

Every small action fights off procrastination. Thus, even the smallest step toward your goal can build momentum. The trick here is to be consistent with your small steps. If you begin to take action, you have successfully beaten procrastination from occurring and you prevent self-sabotage. This will make you feel better and prevent you from delaying your task.

Be Your Own Best Friend

You need to learn not to be so hard on yourself. A large part of self-sabotage that prevents action is when you constantly tell yourself that you are not good enough or incapable of success. You need to stop and think about whether you would say these things to your best friend. Be kinder to yourself because being harsh will hurt you so much more. You would not do it to anyone else, so why do it to yourself?

The more you practice these techniques in your daily life, the easier it will become. Self-sabotaging procrastination needs to be eliminated because not only does it lead to the creation of bad habits, but it also keeps you from progressing. Bringing awareness to self-sabotaging behaviors can be an excellent step in changing your thought patterns and gearing your mind up for success.

CHAPTER 7

ACHIEVING YOUR GOALS —LONG-TERM SUCCESS

Setting long-term goals is an essential step in everyone's personal and professional development. However, many people struggle to achieve their long-term goals due to a common obstacle: procrastination. To achieve your long-term goals and overcome procrastination, you must first learn how to properly define your goals and put strategies in place that ensure that you can achieve them. In this chapter, we will go through the concept of S.M.A.R.T. goals and how you can use them to your advantage to become the best possible version of yourself over time.

DEFINING S.M.A.R.T. GOALS AND REFINING THEM OVER TIME

The first step in overcoming procrastination and achieving long-term goals is to define goals that are specific, measurable, achievable, relevant, and time-bound (S.M.A.R.T.). The acronym is handy because it reminds you of what is truly important when setting goals.

- **S**pecific goals provide clarity and focus on what needs to be accomplished.
- **M**easurable goals allow you to track progress and stay motivated.
- **A**chievable goals set realistic expectations and prevent you from becoming overwhelmed.
- **R**elevant goals are aligned with your values and aspirations, making them meaningful and worth pursuing.
- **T**ime-bound goals have clear deadlines, which create a sense of urgency and accountability.

Defining your long-term goals in this manner can keep you focused, motivated, and accountable during the entire process of goal achievement. However, it is important to note that goal-setting is not a once-off thing. Everything changes over time—including what we want out of life. Whether we are thinking about our personal or professional lives, our priorities change, and our goals will change as well. Changing your goals does not make you fickle. In fact, it just shows that you understand yourself better over time and are dedicated to setting realistic and relevant goals that always consider your improvement, growth, and desires.

Thus, you should always take the time to reevaluate your S.M.A.R.T. goals after you have defined them. In the professional sphere, most people evaluate their goals annually to ensure that it still aligns with their growth. However, if procrastination is your main concern, you should aim to evaluate your goals every quarter. In this way, it serves as a reminder of what you are working toward and will allow you to track your progress. Measurable goals will allow you to do this without hassle because the metrics are already in place. If you find that you have met your target for a quarter, you will be motivated to continue to the next target. On the flip side, should you find yourself falling behind, you know which areas deserve more attention.

S.M.A.R.T. goals work to cut down procrastination and provide a clear plan for achieving long-term goals. If you use them as a part of your strategy, you will undoubtedly have a clear path to follow. They are clearly defined, with all the details there for you to follow. This is why it is good to consult your long-term goals often to ensure that you reach your targets and maintain the correct pace.

BREAKING DOWN GOALS INTO CONCRETE ACTIONS AND PLANNING THEIR ACHIEVEMENT

When you have established your S.M.A.R.T. goals, the next step is to break them down into smaller, manageable tasks. This helps you overcome the overwhelming feeling of trying to do something big or challenging that often leads to procrastination. By breaking your goals down into smaller steps, you create a clear roadmap that guides your actions and prevents you from feeling stuck or unsure about where to begin. In this way, you can spring into action without having any excuses as to why you cannot begin pursuing your goals.

To break down your goals effectively, start by identifying the major milestones or outcomes you need to achieve. Then, working backward, break those milestones into smaller, actionable tasks. Each task should be clear, specific, and achievable within a reasonable timeframe. For example, if you wish to learn a new language within a year, you can break it down into smaller, actionable tasks. These could include giving yourself a week to find a suitable class or online course that you can register for, learning the basics within two months, and finding someone to converse with to improve fluency in six months. By focusing on one task at a time, you create a sense of progress and build momentum. In turn, you can overcome procrastination because the steps are already laid out and you will be motivated with every task you complete.

In addition to breaking down goals, it is crucial to create an overall plan for their achievement. Planning involves determining the necessary resources that you will require, allocating adequate time, and organizing your schedule to accommodate the tasks required to reach your goals. To use the example of learning a new language again, the resources you require may be a tutor, course, or books that will help you learn the language, figure out which time is best for you to study, and ensure that you schedule in your study time each day. Developing a structured plan like this not only helps you stay organized but also provides a framework for you to follow, reducing the likelihood of procrastination. When you have a well-defined plan in place, you are more likely to take consistent action toward your goals because the steps are already set out for you to follow.

If you define your S.M.A.R.T. goals, break them down into smaller tasks, and create a clear plan to achieve each task; you will be well on your way to achieving your long-term goals. Procrastination will only rear its head if you choose to delay a task. However, by creating a plan that fits into your current schedule, there really shouldn't be any reasons for delays besides unexpected occurrences or emergencies that come up. If this does happen, you can always pick up where you left off.

MONITORING PROGRESS AND CELEBRATING MILESTONE ACCOMPLISHMENTS

In order to stay motivated when pursuing your goals—and to avoid giving procrastination a gap to slip in—it is essential to monitor your progress. Regularly tracking your progress allows you to stay accountable, ensuring that you are following the plan that you originally set out. In addition, tracking your progress provides valuable feedback on your efforts and helps you identify where you are not sticking to your targets. You can then assess the plan that you set up to complete the tasks needed to achieve your long-term goals to see exactly where you are having issues. It gives you a chance to adapt your strategies and improve your approach to your targets.

An effective way to monitor progress is by using a goal-tracking system. By breaking down goals into smaller tasks it is much easier to track your progress, as you can check off completed tasks one by one. Depending on what you are comfortable with, this can be as simple as a checklist or as sophisticated as a digital app. The key is to find a method that works for you. When you are able to visually see your progress, it can make a massive difference. People often find it surprising to see how much they have truly accomplished. Not only does it make them feel better and provide a boost in self-confidence, but it also motivates them to keep following the plan.

It is also necessary to celebrate when you reach milestones. Achieving your long-term goals often requires time, effort, and resilience. It's important to acknowledge and reward yourself along the way when you meet your targets. Take the time to celebrate and appreciate your progress when you complete a significant task because you deserve it. Overcoming procrastination is no small feat and sticking to your plan and achieving your goals is definitely worth celebrating. This celebration can take the form of treating yourself, sharing your accomplishments with others, or simply taking a moment to reflect on how far you have come. By celebrating your achievements, you reinforce the positive behaviors you have developed and build momentum to continue moving forward.

SUSTAINING COMMITMENT AND ADAPTING TO CHALLENGES ALONG THE JOURNEY

When things are going well and you are meeting your targets and achieving your goals, it is easy to stay on track and overcome procrastination. However, remaining committed to your goals can be challenging over time, especially when faced with obstacles or setbacks. Therefore, it is essential to develop strategies for sustaining commitment and adapting to challenges along the journey.

Maintain Accountability

One effective strategy is to find accountability partners or support systems to keep you motivated to pursue your goals. Sharing your goals and progress with trusted friends, family members, or mentors can provide invaluable support and encouragement. Accountability partners can help keep you on track, provide fresh perspectives, and offer guidance during challenging times. By involving others in your journey, you create a sense of responsibility and increase your commitment to your goals. This makes it harder to succumb to procrastination when the temptation strikes.

Self-Reflection

Another crucial aspect of sustaining commitment is self-reflection and self-care. Take the time to understand your motivations and underlying reasons for pursuing your goals. When you pause to reflect on your values and aspirations, it can help reignite your passion and remind you of the importance of staying committed. You should also prioritize self-care activities that rejuvenate and recharge you. When you take care of your physical and mental well-being, you are better equipped to overcome procrastination and maintain focus on your long-term goals.

Adaptability

Adapting to challenges is an inevitable part of the journey toward long-term success. Unexpected obstacles, changing circumstances, or new opportunities may require you to adjust your plans or even reconsider your goals entirely. Flexibility and adaptability are crucial for overcoming procrastination in the face of challenges. Embrace change as an opportunity for growth and learning, and be willing to modify your approach when necessary. By being able to adapt, you can maintain momentum and continue progressing toward your long-term goals confidently.

It is possible to achieve your goals and overcome procrastination if you put the right strategies in place. Taking the time to define your goals and formulating a solid plan to achieve them is the best place to start. As a result, no matter what happens in the short term, you have a plan that you can adapt to meet your requirements while also keeping you on track for success.

CHAPTER 8

MANAGING STRESS AND ANXIETY RELATED TO PROCRASTINATION

Procrastination, stress, and anxiety are part of a vicious cycle. When we procrastinate, our stress levels rise when we begin to feel overwhelmed and realize the magnitude of the task ahead when we give ourselves less time. Procrastination can also fuel anxiety when the fear of not meeting expectations or experiencing negative outcomes grows. In addition, when we are stressed and anxious, there is less desire to continue with tasks, thus leading to procrastination. If we continue to allow this cycle to continue, we will never be able to manage any of these conditions. This is why it is crucial to develop techniques and skills that can help you manage the stress and anxiety associated with procrastination.

STRESS MANAGEMENT TECHNIQUES

Stress management is something that we have all had to implement at some point or the other. Both work and personal issues can give rise to stress and it can greatly impact our performance in everyday life. In addition, chronic stress can also affect our physical health, which will also affect our ability to perform at our best. Couple these mental and physical symptoms with procrastination and it usually results in the inability to get anything done. To avoid these negative effects of stress, it is crucial to implement stress management techniques into your regular routines. Even if you do not feel overly stressed, being able to find outlets to deal with it will help you remain calm and productive no matter what you do. Here are some great options for managing stress related to procrastination.

Deep Breathing

Engaging in deep breathing exercises or practicing relaxation techniques, such as progressive muscle relaxation or meditation, can help calm the mind and reduce stress levels. By taking a few minutes each day to focus on your breath and release tension, you can reduce any feelings of stress that you may have. Different people have different approaches to this technique. Some prefer to start their days with it to instill clarity and focus for everything that lies ahead, while some prefer to end their day with this technique to remove feelings of stress that have accumulated during the day. They both work equally well and you can decide when and where is the best time for you. In all honesty, practicing deep breathing whenever you feel stressed can help ground you and bring you back to the task at hand with a calmer, more focused mind.

Physical Activity

Although it always seems like there is never enough time, engaging in regular physical exercise can provide the ideal outlet for stress and anxiety. Exercise releases endorphins, which are natural mood elevators, and helps reduce stress hormones (Anderson & Shivakumar, 2013). Incorporating physical activity into your routine, such as walking, jogging, or yoga, can help alleviate stress and improve overall well-being.

Creative Outlets

Another excellent technique to deal with stress is to find creative outlets that will not only calm you down but also provide a bit of fun in your life. Whether you choose music, art, or dancing, it is a great alternative if physical activity is not something that you enjoy. Creative outlets spark joy and allow your stress to dissipate when you focus on more enjoyable activities. Furthermore, learning new skills, even in creative fields, is good practice in terms of personal growth and keeping your brain active.

Time Management Techniques

We have spoken about how time management techniques can help with procrastination and decrease stress. However, it is worth reiterating because it is one of the best things you can do to handle stress in your life. If you work on the strategies to better manage your time, not only will your stress levels decrease, but you will find that you have more time to put stress management practices in place. For example, if you manage your time effectively at work, you have enough time to go to the gym or an art class after work. Everything ties in together beautifully if you just take the time to put everything into motion.

Supportive Networks

If you have people around you who are supportive, it means that you have people to talk to when you are stressed. More often than not, simply speaking to someone you trust such as a friend, family member, partner, or mentor can lower your stress levels. It gives you the opportunity to voice your concerns out loud and rationalize your thoughts. This can make a huge difference in finding solutions to problems and making you feel more in control of situations.

STRATEGIES FOR DEALING WITH ANXIETY

Dealing with anxiety related to procrastination requires specific strategies to address the underlying fears and concerns that you may have. These fears and concerns are what feed your anxiety, making it impossible to complete tasks. Strategies that deal with anxiety focus more on thought patterns and self-reflection, as these are the best ways to address those underlying fears. Here are some of the best strategies for dealing with anxiety.

Identify Negative Thought Patterns

Anxiety often stems from negative thoughts and self-doubt. Take the time to identify the negative thoughts associated with your procrastination habits and challenge them. You can do this by writing them down and questioning their validity. Where are they coming from? Do they originate from past experiences? Is it real? Once you work through these negative thoughts, you can then start replacing negative thoughts with positive and realistic affirmations. This will help to promote self-confidence and motivate you to continue working on your tasks and leaving the negativity behind.

Set Realistic Expectations

Other causes of anxiety-induced procrastination are perfectionism and high expectations. If you always aim for perfection, you could have too-high expectations of yourself, which causes you to stop working on a task until you believe that you can achieve that level of work. You need to accept that perfection is not always immediately attainable. Furthermore, aiming to always do your best when completing tasks is much better than expecting a flawless result. If you experience a challenge whilst working on a task, the outcome might be better than having a process that goes smoothly because you will learn more along the way.

Break Up Tasks Into Manageable Steps

Breaking tasks down into smaller, manageable steps can reduce anxiety and make the overall task more approachable. By focusing on one step at a time, you can alleviate the overwhelming, anxious feeling that often accompanies procrastination. Furthermore, as you complete each step of the task, you will feel more in control of the situation and experience less fear.

Set Boundaries

Another reason why anxiety takes over is that we do not set clear boundaries. You have to know when to draw the line and not take on more work to please or impress others. The act of setting boundaries comes from a deep understanding of yourself and your capabilities. It is okay to say "no" every once in a while. It will allow you to work well on what you can and take much-needed breaks between tasks. Just because you are good at what you do, does not mean that you are solely responsible for everything. Remember that.

SELF-CARE PRACTICES TO REDUCE STRESS

Self-care is essential for reducing stress, anxiety, and maintaining overall well-being. Most people look at self-care as a waste of time or think of it as a selfish act when there is so much else to do. However, by incorporating self-care into your routines, you can effectively manage stress related to procrastination and promote a healthier mindset. In turn, you present your best possible self when you take on tasks. This ensures that you are not carrying any stress, anxiety, or other burdens with you that will hinder you from productive work.

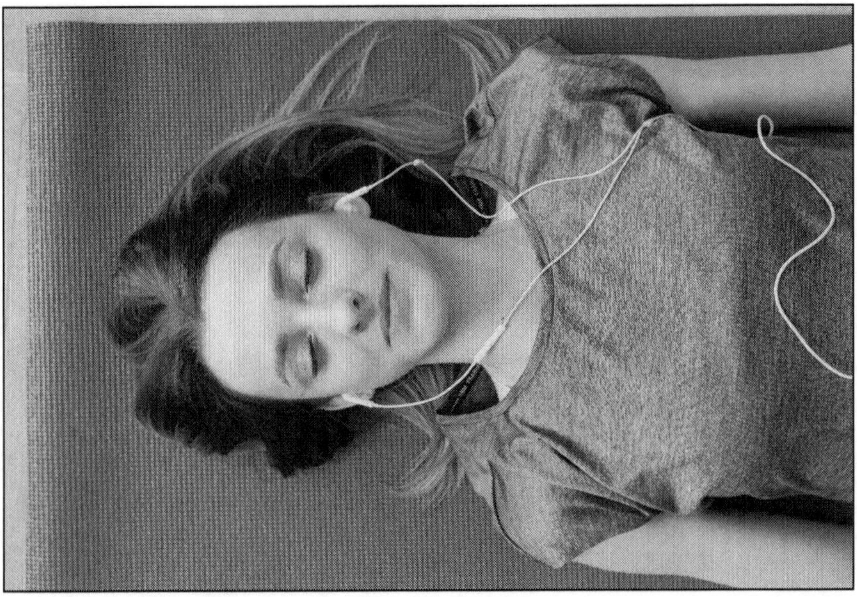

Practice Mindfulness

Engaging in mindfulness activities, such as meditation or mindful breathing, can help you stay present and reduce stress. Taking a few moments each day to focus on the present moment can alleviate anxiety and improve your ability to focus on the task at hand. Mindfulness is also a great form of self-care as it encourages you to stay present, be mindful of your thoughts, and not worry about things in the past or future that cause anxiety.

Prioritize Sleep

Many of us do not get enough sleep as we try to get everything done in the limited time we have. Furthermore, binge-watching television series and social media are huge causes of not getting enough rest at night. A lack of sleep can contribute to increased stress levels and make any anxiety you experience feel worse. You must prioritize sleep by establishing a consistent sleep routine and creating a conducive environment for quality rest. A well-rested mind and body are better equipped to handle stress and overcome procrastination than a tired one.

Engage in Activities You Enjoy

Making time for activities and hobbies that bring you joy and help you relax is great for self-care. Not only does it make you feel better but it acts as a form of stress relief. In addition, it provides a much-needed break from the pressures of procrastination. These activities can include anything from spending quality time with your family to going on a hike to reconnect with nature. You know what brings peace to your mind and soul, but if you don't, go out there and find what does!

STRATEGIES FOR ADDRESSING EMOTIONAL OBSTACLES IN PROCRASTINATION

Emotional obstacles, such as fear, self-doubt, and lack of motivation, can significantly contribute to stress and anxiety related to procrastination. Addressing these emotional obstacles is crucial for managing stress and increasing productivity. Much like dealing with anxiety, addressing emotional obstacles involves self-reflection. You have to understand your emotions better to be able to identify the obstacles they present. To do this, you should be more observant of your emotions and when they arise. Keeping a journal to note this down will allow you to reflect on them at the end of the day. You can evaluate what triggers certain emotions and the effects it has on your thoughts and actions.

It is important to note that both positive and negative emotions can cause procrastination. Positive emotions can tempt you away from tasks while negative emotions can cause an avoidance of tasks. Thus, they both pose emotional obstacles. It is important that you do not ignore positive emotions when you are trying to assess the resulting thoughts and actions. In addition, learning to regulate your emotions better can also help you better deal with procrastination. Emotional regulation involves many of the strategies that we have already mentioned such as mindfulness, healthy coping mechanisms, and self-compassion.

If you address your emotions as they arise, you can stop them from becoming obstacles and gain better control of your actions. This means that you can nip procrastination in the bud and get rid of the emotions that do not serve you. It also means that you have a better handle on how your emotions affect all your actions and not just those involved in task completion.

CHAPTER 9

DEVELOPING HABITS OF SELF-DISCIPLINE AND CONSISTENCY OVER TIME

Self-discipline and consistency are essential traits for overcoming procrastination and achieving long-term success. They involve the ability to stay focused, motivated, and committed to our goals, even when faced with challenges or distractions. Contrary to popular belief, this does not mean that you have to remain rigid and exhibit strict discipline to achieve your goals. It means that you have to remain consistent in your pursuit, be adaptable, and develop self-discipline to keep you on track. In this chapter, we will explore the importance of self-discipline and consistency and strategies to help you develop them.

UNDERSTANDING THE IMPORTANCE OF SELF-DISCIPLINE AND CONSISTENCY

In order to develop self-discipline and consistency, you first have to understand them. Self-discipline refers to the ability to control and regulate oneself, maintaining focus and avoiding distractions or temptations that hinder progress in any way. It involves making conscious choices aligned with long-term goals, even if they require effort or sacrifice in the short term. For example, spending 30 minutes at the end of the day to plan ahead for tomorrow instead of watching television will make the next day run smoother. In this case, self-discipline makes you forgo the immediate gratification of watching television and allows you to focus on a task that will make your day run smoother in the future.

Consistency, on the other hand, refers to the ability to take regular, persistent action toward our goals, building habits that support our desired outcomes. When you are able to repeat an action consistently and can carry it out automatically, that means that it has successfully become a habit. Therefore, you need to ensure that the strategies and techniques you use to overcome procrastination become habits over time.

Self-discipline and consistency are crucial for overcoming procrastination because they provide the structure and motivation needed to take regular action. They help us resist the temptation to delay or avoid tasks and ensure that we stay on track toward achieving our goals. These are two characteristics that are exhibited by professional athletes and it helps them keep their end goal in mind while they train. By developing habits of self-discipline and consistency, we can also increase our productivity, maintain momentum, and make significant progress over time just like these athletes do.

STRATEGIES FOR DEVELOPING SELF-DISCIPLINE

Self-discipline is a great skill to develop, but many people make a mistake in what it entails. This leads to them not fully developing the skill in its entirety. Self-discipline is not just one thing—it is made up of three different elements. You get cognitive, emotional, and behavioral self-discipline. Thus, instead of just developing behavioral self-discipline, which allows you to control your behaviors and actions, you also need to be able to alter your thoughts (cognitive self-discipline) and recognize when you are overwhelmed by your emotions (emotional self-discipline).

Thus, to develop self-discipline you must be aware of your thoughts, emotions, and actions. Sound familiar? That's because multiple strategies that we have discussed thus far require the same awareness. Solid strategies for developing self-discipline include the following:

- Identify your motivation for pursuing your goals.
- Don't make excuses or rationalize them.
- Develop solid plans that provide clear direction and help you achieve your goals.
- Always be mindful of thoughts, emotions, and behaviors, because then you can determine which serve you and which are unproductive.

- Identify the bad habits that prevent you from achieving your goals and replace them with good habits that are productive.
- Hold yourself accountable either by creating time-defined targets or by having an accountability partner.
- Reward yourself to create positive associations with maintaining self-discipline.

Developing self-discipline does not happen overnight and you should not be too hard on yourself if you slip up every once in a while. You have to constantly work on the strategies so that they become automatic in everything that you do. Over time, you will find yourself naturally regulating your thoughts, emotions, and behaviors in such a way that others will admire your discipline to achieve your goals. You just have to remember to keep practicing your strategies so that you do not fall into bad habits once again. However, if you are committed to making a change, you will naturally keep trying until you succeed.

CULTIVATING CONSISTENCY IN ACTIONS

Consistency is key to developing habits and making progress toward your goals. With consistency, you aim to repeat the same actions so that you can achieve the desired outcome. However, being consistent does not automatically translate into monotony. This is a common problem that people face while trying to remain consistent—they get bored with the same routine. What they fail to realize is that it does not have to be this way. Yes, you need to be consistent with your actions, but that does not necessarily mean that you have to do exactly the same thing at the same time every day. For example, consider people who have a goal to improve their health. This may entail a healthy eating plan and increasing physical activity. What makes people give up when following this goal could be boredom which, in turn, will lead to procrastination. They do not feel motivated to go to the gym every morning or prepare their meals every night.

However, this boredom can be dealt with by formulating a schedule that will allow you to remain consistent but eliminate the boredom. So, you can schedule time for the tasks associated with achieving your goals, but you can vary when, where, and how you approach it. If we look at the health goal again, you can vary physical activity in terms of gym, hiking, yoga, and spin classes. They would all be on different days and at different times, but they help you achieve your overall goal. Likewise, you can choose to prepare your meals or ingredients on a Sunday for the week ahead, and you can mix and match ingredients every day. Therefore, you are still consistently working toward your goal and avoiding procrastination by having a solid plan that enables you to adapt along the way.

The next thing you should aim to do to cultivate consistency is to always set realistic expectations. There is always the temptation to aim bigger when things are going well. As much as it is not a bad thing to want to do more, you must always be realistic. Ensure that your goals and tasks are realistic and do not mess up the good system you have going. It's no point in trying to do more if it interferes with a schedule that is working well and with which you are making progress. If it begins to cause you to fall behind on other tasks, then it is worth re-evaluating and adjusting to ensure that it does not cause you to lose your consistency.

MANAGING SETBACKS AND REBOUNDING AFTER A PERIOD OF LACKING SELF-DISCIPLINE

Setbacks happen—they are unavoidable. No matter how diligent you are and how many strategies you have in place, they will occur. Sometimes, it could be a completely random event that may throw you off schedule, while at others, it could just be a lack of self-discipline. Whichever one it may be, rebounding from these setbacks is the most important thing that you can do. You must not allow setbacks to be the thing that derails all the progress you have made in overcoming procrastination. If you do experience a setback, you need to use your resilience to get back into your routine of self-discipline and consistency.

Here are some tips on managing setbacks and rebounding effectively:

- **Reflect on the reasons for the setback.** As much as you are in a rush to get back into your routine, take the time necessary to reflect on the reasons behind the lapse in self-discipline. Identify any triggers or obstacles that contributed to the setback. If you understand the root causes of your setback, it can help you develop strategies to overcome them in the future. In addition, you can also put procedures in place that can help you avoid a similar setback altogether.

- **Practice self-compassion.** Be kind and forgiving to yourself when you experience a setback. It is easy to feel defeated when things go wrong, but this is where your growth mindset can come in handy. Acknowledge that setbacks happen to everyone and that they are opportunities for growth. Instead of dwelling on past failures and allowing them to become reasons for procrastination, focus on what you can do differently moving forward.
- **Revisit your goals and recommit.** You need to remind yourself of the importance of your goals and the reasons why you want to achieve them. It is possible to use setbacks as a chance to reaffirm your commitment and spark your motivation once again. Remember that a setback is not a failure, it is a challenge that can make your success seem all the more sweeter!

INTEGRATING SELF-DISCIPLINE INTO YOUR LIFE

To make self-discipline a lasting habit, it needs to be integrated into your daily life. Besides having clear, realistic goals that are broken down into manageable tasks, you also need to have a clear strategy as to how you are going to demonstrate self-discipline and consistency every day.

Here's how you can do this:

- **Remove temptations that will weaken your self-discipline.** You know what your strengths and weaknesses are. Thus, you should aim to remove the temptations that you know will definitely cause setbacks.

- **Consistency is key.** If you want self-discipline to become a habit, you need to practice it every day. Think of it as a skill or talent that you would like to master. You can only master it if you set aside time for practice—self-discipline is the same.
- **Create the right mindset** if you want to remain disciplined. This entails embracing challenges, knowing that they will strengthen your approach, and not being afraid of setbacks. If you have the right mindset, you will always look at ways to continue on your path and not turn your back on achieving your goals.
- **Develop good habits to aid your self-discipline.** When you get rid of temptations and bad habits, you have room for good habits to form. When trying to integrate self-discipline into your life, develop good habits that will help make this easier. For example, turn off email and message notifications that cause distractions throughout your day, or leave your phone far away from your bed to prevent scrolling before bedtime.
- **Always have a contingency plan.** If you are not able to exhibit consistency or self-discipline on any given day, what do you do? If you have a backup plan in place, you make it possible to rebound faster and get back to your routine without spending time trying to find a solution when it occurs.

CHAPTER 10

STRATEGIES FOR MANAGING DEADLINES AND PREVENTING PROCRASTINATION

Deadlines come in all shapes and forms—and with them come all types of emotions. Some deadlines are not taken seriously, so we tend to procrastinate until they get closer and we have to deal with them. Others seem daunting from the start, filling us with fear, stress, and anxiety that can affect our performance and the outcomes of our tasks. People can even feel more productive because they find that a deadline makes them work faster. However, that is not always the case, as faster does not always translate into better. This is why we need to learn how to manage deadlines effectively and prevent procrastination from affecting our true potential. If we allow procrastination to affect how we perceive deadlines, we will not produce the best results as our focus will be on how we feel and not on the task. Thus, it is vital that we put strategies in place to manage how we approach deadlines and keep procrastination from taking over.

UNDERSTANDING THE IMPORTANCE OF DEADLINE MANAGEMENT

First of all, what do you think of when you hear the word *deadline*? The first word that comes to your mind is actually a good indicator of how deadlines make you feel. Some words that are common are *stressful*, *high pressure*, and *expectations*, to name a few. However, thinking of deadlines in this way will taint the way your brain approaches them. It will constantly think of unpleasantness and not see the actual gift that a deadline is. A deadline is nothing more than a goal. It may be set by someone else, but the intention is the same—it is a short-term goal that you are working toward. Thus, just like how you would break down goals into manageable tasks and then set out a plan for these tasks, deadline management is the process of planning, organizing, and executing tasks to ensure they are completed on time.

Given how most of us work at the moment trying to frantically meet deadlines, we either meet the deadline by rushing through the tasks, ask for extensions to ensure that everything is perfect, or submit our work late despite the deadline. However, meeting your deadline should not always be a mad dash to the finish. We have discussed the importance of time management earlier in the book, and putting those strategies in place can greatly assist in meeting your deadlines better. This is crucial as effective deadline management is essential for three reasons:

1. Accountability

Deadlines provide accountability by setting clear expectations and consequences for the timely completion of tasks. When you know you have a looming deadline, you usually kick into gear and start working on the task. Deadlines create a sense of urgency and responsibility, motivating individuals to take action. If you procrastinate, you will be held accountable by the person who set the deadline, including yourself.

2. Productivity

By setting deadlines, individuals are encouraged to prioritize tasks and allocate their time and resources efficiently. This focus on productivity increases the likelihood of achieving goals and meeting project milestones. It is the reason why deadlines can actually be your partner in overcoming procrastination instead of being the reason for your procrastination.

3. Reputation and Credibility

When you are able to consistently meet deadlines, you demonstrate reliability and professionalism to those you work with. It enhances your reputation and builds trust among colleagues, clients, and stakeholders because they know that they can rely on you to get the task done.

Thus, if you can manage your deadlines effectively, you have the ability to be productive and will have a reputation of credibility and reliability that everyone will appreciate. This will boost your self-confidence and give you the motivation needed to maintain your deadlines.

PLANNING AND ORGANIZING WORK TO MEET DEADLINES

In order to meet deadlines, you need to plan accordingly and be organized. This entails effective time management that will allow your schedule to run smoothly. Most of the steps that you need to follow to do this have been covered already but to highlight their importance to deadline management specifically, we will go through them briefly.

You need to start by analyzing the project you have been given and break it up into smaller, manageable tasks that you can easily handle and track. Once you have a list of tasks, you can then start prioritizing, planning, and organizing them into your schedule so that they will be completed by your deadline. This is the most important part of deadline management as you need to assess how much time is needed for each task. In order to do this, you need an understanding of what resources you require, whether you are working alone or are reliant on team members, and whether you have enough space for contingency plans should something get delayed. Knowing your limitations, being aware of your strengths and weaknesses, and having a good understanding of your schedule will help you come up with solid plans to meet your deadlines.

There are also several digital tools available that can help you with planning and organizing your work. These tools help you visualize your deadlines, set reminders, and allocate time for each task. When you have a clear image in front of you of your deadlines and each of your respective tasks, it can help you stay focused and organized. You will know exactly what you are working on and when it needs to be completed. Digital tools also have the advantage of automated notifications and collaborative features that help teams stay on target and maintain their deadlines while supporting each other.

PREVENTING PROCRASTINATION AND ADDRESSING POTENTIAL COMPLICATIONS

There are several common causes that can hinder our ability to meet our deadlines effectively—procrastination is just one of them. If we know how to address these complications, we have a better shot at staying on schedule and meeting our deadlines. Let's take a look at the most common challenges that we face when it comes to achieving our deadlines.

1. Poor Time Management

If you cannot manage your time properly, you will be unable to achieve any of your goals, tasks, or deadlines. Therefore, time management is imperative to schedule your tasks in a way that ensures that they will be completed on time. You can even overestimate how long it would take you to complete a task to allow time for unexpected delays. In this way, if you finish earlier than estimated, you can just adapt your schedule and move all your other tasks up accordingly.

2. Unrealistic Expectations

Setting unrealistic expectations can lead to missed deadlines and increased stress and anxiety. It often occurs when people underestimate the time and effort required to complete tasks. Unrealistic expectations can also arise from a lack of experience. If you don't really know how long it would take to complete a specific task, you could underestimate and try to pursue an unrealistic goal. This is why if you are uncertain, it is good to consult with others with more experience. It will give you a better idea of what a realistic timeframe would look like instead of guessing. Furthermore, if you push yourself to meet unrealistic expectations, you will find yourself in this position more often as people will use it as a metric of your capabilities.

3. Lack of Prioritization

Not knowing how to prioritize can cause a lot of problems—not only for your deadlines, but for all your tasks. You need to think about what tasks need to be completed first, what takes the most time to work on, and what you are capable of. The two main pitfalls that people fall into are doing novel tasks first because it appeals to the brain and tackling easy tasks first because it makes them feel productive. This is a problem because you do not take into consideration which tasks are most important. If you do all the new tasks first, the older ones just sit on your to-do list for longer, getting less and less appealing. Likewise, doing all the easy tasks first can also get you in trouble by leaving less time available for harder tasks even though you have been working diligently all along. Therefore, understanding how to prioritize your tasks properly is of the utmost importance to meeting deadlines.

4. Lack of Resources

A lack of necessary resources, such as time, information, or support, can impact your adherence to deadlines. If you don't have what you need to complete a task, you will waste time trying to obtain it while you work. Therefore, it is important that you carefully assess what resources are required during your planning and organizing time. If you identify resources that are lacking, you can speak to the relevant people before you start working on tasks and let them know what you need and by when. This ensures that everyone is on the same page and that you get what you need exactly when you need it, preventing an opportunity for procrastination.

These obstacles will only become a problem if you are unprepared. However, by using the strategies that you have learned thus far regarding overcoming procrastination and effective time management, you have the tools to be prepared to deal with them. You can also ensure that you adhere to deadlines by regularly checking your progress and demonstrating transparency with those you work with. This is where collaborative task management tools also come in handy as they allow you to do this easily. Furthermore, the automatic reminders and project update notifications are great for those who need a little extra motivation.

CHAPTER 11

MAINTAINING MOMENTUM AND SUPPORTING PROGRESS

Now that you know the strategies needed to overcome procrastination, you have to work at keeping them in practice. This is the part that we all struggle with. Everything starts out fine and well, and we are happy with our productivity and progress, but then we start getting complacent—or something happens that completely derails our strategies. Then all the progress we made gets lost as we begin to procrastinate again. Resilience and perseverance are key to sustaining the strategies, but there are also other components that you can work on to sustain your progress and ensure that procrastination cannot creep up on you. The information in this chapter may seem repetitive, but it serves to highlight the important steps that you should follow to overcome procrastination once and for all.

THE POWER OF HABITS TO SUSTAIN CONTINUOUS DEVELOPMENT

Habits are automatic actions and behaviors that we develop over time. Most of the time, we don't notice their development. A good example is having a cup of coffee in the morning. We associate it with feeling awake and starting the day with a boost—without it, we feel as if something is missing from our day. Similarly, we should aim to make the strategies that we use to overcome procrastination habits that we follow. In this way, they become automatic thoughts, actions, and behaviors which do not require effort. Developing new habits is not an easy process as it takes time and consistent practice. However, once you have developed the right habits, there's no chance that you will ever forget them or not act on them because you will feel like something is missing from your day—just like that cup of coffee.

Here are some tips to help you build good habits quickly:

- **Start Small and Be Specific.** When trying to develop a new habit, it's important to start with small steps and be specific about what you want to achieve. Break down the desired behavior into manageable actions that can easily be incorporated into your daily routine. For example, if you want to overcome procrastination that leads you away from exercising daily, you can start with a short 10-minute workout every day. You can slot in these 10 minutes at any time of the day and gradually increase the duration every so often.

- **Create a Trigger.** A trigger is a specific cue or reminder that prompts you to engage in a desired habit. It can be a time of day, a specific location, an object, or an existing routine that serves as a reminder to perform the habit. For example, if you want to develop a habit of using a planner to track your tasks for the day, you can either place a physical planner on your desk where you can see it as soon as you sit down, or you can set a reminder on your digital planner so that it shows up on your screen at the start of the day. These cues trigger your brain and work to remind you to use your planner.

- **Be Consistent.** Consistency is key when developing a new habit or when trying to break a bad habit. Commit to practicing the habit every day or at specific intervals, depending on the habit you're trying to cultivate. For example, if you are working on the negative thought patterns that make you procrastinate at work, you can implement a quick meditation and calm breathing break at certain times during the day. Consistency helps reinforce the habit and makes it easier to stick to over time. Avoid skipping days or making excuses, even if the task seems small or insignificant.
- **Be Patient and Practice Self-Compassion.** Developing new habits takes time and effort. You must not beat yourself up if you slip up every so often. It's important to be patient with yourself and not get discouraged. Instead of criticizing yourself, practice self-compassion and use the setbacks as opportunities to work on your resilience. Remember that developing good habits is a journey, and progress is more important than perfection.

DEALING WITH PROCRASTINATION SETBACKS WITH DETERMINATION

Overcoming procrastination setbacks is a crucial aspect of maintaining momentum in your journey. It is normal to experience setbacks along the way, but it is also essential to approach them with determination and resilience. This is the only way that you can break the habit of thinking that a setback is a failure. A challenge is never a failure but an opportunity to learn and improve yourself. If you can embrace this mindset, you will never procrastinate due to setbacks and will instead, kick into gear and start tackling it. Here are a few reminders of what you should do when you encounter setbacks:

- **Practice Acceptance and Mindfulness.** You need to practice acceptance and mindfulness in order to acknowledge that setbacks are a natural part of the process and avoid self-criticism. You want your focus to stay in the present and on how to overcome the setback. If you allow your mind to wander, you provide an opportunity for procrastination to continue further. Thus, take a moment to bring the focus back to the present moment when you feel yourself being pulled away.
- **Analyze Triggers.** You need to take the time to identify and reflect on the triggers that lead you to procrastinate. This will help you pinpoint the patterns or underlying causes that contribute to your procrastination tendencies. If you understand these triggers, you can tailor the strategies you use to overcome them.
- **Revisit Your Motivation.** Reconnect with your motivation by reminding yourself of the reasons behind your goals. Visualize the positive outcomes that will result from completing your tasks on time. In doing so, you can regain momentum when you lose it.
- **Breaking Tasks Into Smaller Steps.** If you encounter a setback, analyze the task and break it into smaller, more manageable steps, once again taking the setback into consideration. This is critical because it allows you to adapt your approach and it also makes the task less daunting. Both of these factors increase the likelihood of starting and completing it.

Setbacks will happen whether you like it or not. It's how you perceive them and how you deal with them that will make all the difference in your goal to overcome procrastination.

SELF-REFLECTION AND CONTINUOUS IMPROVEMENT TO OPTIMIZE THE PROCESS

Self-reflection is a powerful tool for optimizing the process of overcoming procrastination. By analyzing your behaviors and identifying areas for improvement, you can refine your strategies and increase your chances of success. Self-reflection is essential for any form of growth but it takes a while to get comfortable with the process. It requires you to closely analyze your thoughts and behaviors and confront some truths that you may have not noticed about yourself before. However, no matter how difficult it is, when you can master self-reflection, you gain an entirely new understanding of yourself. This not only makes you a stronger individual but when you know yourself, you know exactly what you are capable of.

To practice self-reflection, you have to first get used to the idea. It is easier to use a journal to track your progress, challenges, and successes than trying to remember it all in your head. In addition, writing down your emotional responses will give you an opportunity to identify areas for you to work on. Emotional regulation is essential to maintaining a calm demeanor, not becoming overwhelmed, and remaining focused on the task at hand. Journaling as a form of self-reflection can also help you recognize all your achievements. We often achieve much more than we notice, but with self-reflection, we can begin to start seeing that we are actually productive. You will also be able to recognize how much the strategies you implement help you achieve much more.

Thus, self-reflection can show you the positives and negatives in your life. Whether you are assessing your personal or professional life, you can use self-reflection as a tool to improve yourself continuously over time. You can learn from past mistakes, identify the areas that need work, and most importantly, find self-confidence and motivation in all your successes.

CREATING A SYSTEM OF ACCOUNTABILITY AND SUPPORT TO MAINTAIN COMMITMENT

We have mentioned accountability a number of times in this book. It is a crucial component to staying committed to any goal—including overcoming procrastination. However, what is also worth noting is that there are several ways to achieve accountability and gain support. The easiest is to get an accountability partner. This is a person who is close to you and whose opinions you value. By informing them of your intention, you have someone who will check up on your progress. You can even take this a step further by sharing your targets with them so that they know what they need to check and when. Your accountability partner must be someone you trust and who is honest enough to call you out if you stray from your goals. You can't pick someone who is going to always give you a break because then you will never be held accountable to your targets.

You can also consider a support group. There are several online groups that offer support to people who wish to improve themselves and accomplish their goals. Not only will these support groups help you stay accountable, but you can also meet like-minded individuals and learn about how they are working to overcome procrastination. In this way, you gain valuable learning experiences, a supportive network, and accountability partners that will motivate you to stay committed to your pursuit of productivity. If this is not something you are comfortable with, you can also use digital tools to hold yourself accountable. There are various tools that will track your progress, send you reminders about targets, and let you know when you achieve a milestone in your goal pursuit.

Keeping the momentum going and staying committed to overcoming procrastination is indeed possible if you have the right attitude. You have to be determined to not give up and remain resilient when things don't go according to plan. All it takes is remembering your strategies and working through the steps once more so that you can adapt your approach. Never think that you cannot do it, because you most definitely can!

CONCLUSION

Procrastination is not something you can erase overnight. Just like the waves of the ocean beat against the shore, it is always there, ebbing and flowing. Sometimes, when your resistance is low and you least expect it, the tide comes sweeping in, pulling you under, leaving you feeling like you are going to drown. However, the trick is to always stand your ground, face the ocean, and don't let the tide take you by surprise. You have to face your procrastination triggers head-on and know when they threaten to pull you under. This is how you will prevent yourself from drowning in tasks, anxiety, self-doubt, and stress.

This book has provided practical strategies to implement in all areas of your life to deal with procrastination. These are the strategies that you can use to help you back onto the shore so that you can place your feet firmly on the ground in the first place. It is then up to you to identify the procrastination triggers that will cause the tide to come in and pull you back under. It is hard work, but the rewards that you will reap are definitely worth it. Effective time management, overcoming mental barriers, and knowing how to deal with stress and anxiety are vital for overcoming procrastination. If ever you find yourself waning in self-discipline or commitment, just imagine how successful you would be without the obstacle of procrastination in your life. This should be enough to motivate you to keep going. It is essential that you stay motivated and committed to fighting procrastination in your life because this is the only way that you will be successful in doing so.

You also have to remember that it's okay to have setbacks—it is a part of life and nobody is perfect. What sets people apart is how they respond to these setbacks. Be determined to constantly learn from them and always question how you can do better. Don't let setbacks erase your hard work because they are not directly indicative of who you are and what you are capable of. Be persistent in your pursuit of productivity and defeating the time opponent that is procrastination! I truly believe that you have it in you to do so and I hope that this book is the catalyst you needed to get started. Just dig your heels in and brace yourself for all the good things to come.

REFERENCES

Anderson, E., & Shivakumar, G. (2013). Effects of Exercise and Physical Activity on Anxiety. *Frontiers in Psychiatry, 4*(27). https://doi.org/10.3389/fpsyt.2013.00027

Boyes, A. (2019, September 29). *Why Depression and Procrastination Are Linked* Psychology Today South Africa. https://www.psychologytoday.com/za/blog/in-practice/201909/why-depression-and-procrastination-are-linked

Carol Dweck: A Summary of The Two Mindsets. (2015, March 2). Farnam Street. https://fs.blog/carol-dweck-mindset/

Dorin, A. (2022, February 3). History of the Eisenhower Matrix. Perfony. https://www.perfony.com/en/history-of-the-eisenhower-matrix/

Girdhar, K., Ola, M., & Sharma, V. (2020). Impact of Academic Procrastination on Academic Performance. *International Journal of Social Science and Humanities Research, 8*(1), 42–47.

Gleeson, B. (2020, August 25). *9 Powerful Ways To Cultivate Extreme Self-Discipline.* Forbes. https://www.forbes.com/sites/brentgleeson/2020/08/25/8-

powerful-ways-to-cultivate-extreme-self-discipline/?sh=7ed96f20182d

Niermann, H. C. M., & Scheres, A. (2014). The relation between procrastination and symptoms of attention-deficit hyperactivity disorder (ADHD) in undergraduate students. *International Journal of Methods in Psychiatric Research, 23*(4), 411–421. https://doi.org/10.1002/mpr.1440

O'Donovan, K. (2021, April 19). *8 Dreadful Effects of Procrastination That Can Destroy Your Life*. Lifehack; Lifehack. https://www.lifehack.org/articles/productivity/8-ways-procrastination-can-destroy-your-life.html

Shatz, I. (2019). *Why people procrastinate: The psychology and causes of procrastination*. Solving Procrastination. https://solvingprocrastination.com/why-people-procrastinate/

IMAGE REFERENCES

Breakingpic. (2015). Pen on to Do List Paper [Image]. *Pexels.* https://www.pexels.com/photo/pen-calendar-to-do-checklist-3243/

Gouw, T. (2016). man wearing white top using MacBook [Image]. *Unsplash*. https://unsplash.com/photos/1K9T5YiZ2WU

Grabowska, K. (2020). Tranquil woman resting on yoga mat in earphones at home [Image]. *Pexels*. https://www.pexels.com/photo/tranquil-woman-resting-on-yoga-mat-in-earphones-at-home-4498187/

Heyerdahl, C. (2016). [Silver imac with keyboard and trackpad inside room photo] [Image]. *Unsplash.* https://unsplash.com/photos/KE0nC8-58MQ

Janssens, E. (2017). white ceramic mug with coffee on top of a planner [Image]. *Unsplash.* https://unsplash.com/photos/aQfhbxailCs

Jordan, B. (2020). brown wooden blocks on white surface [Image]. *Unsplash.* https://unsplash.com/photos/JD0D-lReHFE

Jordan, B. (2021). brown wooden blocks on white surface [Image]. *Unsplash.* https://unsplash.com/photos/q8ZgKZutttE

krakenimages. (2021). man in white dress shirt sitting beside woman in black long sleeve shirt [Image]. *Unsplash.* https://unsplash.com/photos/376KN_ISplE

Krukau, Y. (2021). A Woman in Black Blazer Sitting at the Desk with Documents [Image]. *Pexels.* https://www.pexels.com/photo/a-woman-in-black-blazer-sitting-at-the-desk-with-documents-7640447/

Magnet.me. (2020). woman in black long sleeve shirt using macbook [Image]. *Unsplash.* https://unsplash.com/photos/LDcC7aCWVlo

Miroshnichenko, T. (2020). Close-Up Photo of Vintage Alarm Clocks [Image]. *Pexels.* https://www.pexels.com/photo/close-up-photo-of-vintage-alarm-clocks-8327971/

Neel, A. (2019). Photo of Man Leaning on Wooden Table [Image]. *Pexels.* https://www.pexels.com/photo/photo-of-man-leaning-on-wooden-table-3132388/

Nepriakhina, D. (2021). green leather tablet case beside black pen [Image]. *Unsplash*. https://unsplash.com/photos/wcomiVt0w1c

Overgoor, R. (2021). black and silver pen on gray textile [Image]. *Unsplash*. https://unsplash.com/photos/EdKCckXXRCI

RDNE Stock project. (2021). Calendar with Deadline Reminder [Image]. *Pexels*. https://www.pexels.com/photo/calendar-with-deadline-reminder-7580856/

Shvets, A. (2020). Woman Holding A Paper [Image]. *Pexels*. https://www.pexels.com/photo/woman-holding-a-paper-3727463/

theblowup. (2020). [*Text photo - Free Motivation Image*] [Image]. *Unsplash*. https://unsplash.com/photos/UN4PadDppAU

ThisIsEngineering. (2020). Woman In Black Tank Top [Image]. *Pexels*. https://www.pexels.com/photo/woman-in-black-tank-top-3861962/

Tran, B. (2017). Inspirational Quotes On A Planner [Image]. *Pexels*. https://www.pexels.com/photo/inspirational-quotes-on-a-planner-636243/

Wilkinson, S. (2021). happy new year greeting card [Image]. *Unsplash*. https://unsplash.com/photos/EDJKEXFbzHA

Printed in Great Britain
by Amazon

36051499R00057